W9-COY-613

Profiles of the Presidents

JAMES A. GARFIELD

★ ★ ★

Profiles of the Presidents

JAMES A. GARFIELD

by Robin S. Doak

Content Advisers: Debbie Weinkamer and Sue Muehlhauser, Interpreters/Researchers, and Edith Serkownek, former Site Manager, James A. Garfield National Historic Site, Mentor, Ohio

Reading Adviser: Dr. Linda D. Labbo, Department of Reading Education, College of Education, The University of Georgia

Compass Point Books
3109 West 50th Street, #115
Minneapolis, MN 55410

Visit Compass Point Books on the Internet at *www.compasspointbooks.com*
or e-mail your request to *custserv@compasspointbooks.com*

Editors: E. Russell Primm, Emily J. Dolbear, Melissa McDaniel, and Catherine Neitge
Photo Researcher: Svetlana Zhurkina
Photo Selector: Linda S. Koutris
Designer: The Design Lab
Cartographer: XNR Productions, Inc.

Library of Congress Cataloging-in-Publication Data
Doak, Robin S. (Robin Santos), 1963–
  James A. Garfield / by Robin S. Doak.
    p. cm.— (Profiles of the presidents)
Includes bibliographical references and index.
Contents: Last of the log cabin presidents—A young scholar—War hero and politician—Rising to the
top—Days in the White House—A violent end to a brilliant career.
  ISBN 0-7565-0267-5 (hardcover)
 1. Garfield, James A. (James Abram), 1831–1881—Juvenile literature. 2. Presidents—United States—
Biography—Juvenile literature. [1. Garfield, James A. (James Abram), 1831–1881. 2. Presidents.] I.
Title. II. Series.
  E687 .D67 2003
  973.8'4'092—dc21   2002009999

Table of Contents

★ ★ ★

*NOTE: In this book, words that are defined in the glossary are in **bold** the first time they appear in the text.*

Last of the Log-Cabin Presidents

★ ★ ★

James A. Garfield had little time to show what kind of a president he would be. He had been in office less than four months when he was cut down by an **assassin's**

Garfield's presidency ▶
was cut short by an
assassin's bullet.

bullet. He died eleven weeks later. Vice President Chester A. Arthur then became president.

Few people today remember James Garfield. He is one of the four so-called Forgotten Presidents of the late 1800s. The other three were Chester Arthur, Benjamin Harrison, and Rutherford B. Hayes.

▲ *James Garfield served with distinction in the Union army during the Civil War.*

Although forgotten by history, Garfield accomplished much before he became president. He was the perfect example of a self-made man. Born in a log cabin in Ohio, Garfield's background was one of the poorest among U.S. presidents. From an early age, however, he showed a keen interest in education. First, he worked hard to put himself through college. Then, after graduating, he worked as a teacher, a politician, and a lawyer. He was also an excellent officer for the Union army during the Civil War.

During the short time he spent in the White House,

Garfield worked to make the president's role stronger. He also began to change the way people were hired for government jobs. By the time he died, Garfield had already taken steps that would save the government millions of dollars.

Garfield rose from poverty to the presidency. ▲ Unfortunately, we cannot know what else he might have done as president.

During his time as a U.S. representative from Ohio and as president, Garfield served the United States well. His story is one of overcoming poverty to rise to the top.

A Young Scholar

★ ★ ★

James Abram Garfield was born on November 19, 1831, in a log cabin in Orange Township, Ohio. About two years before James was born, his parents—Abram

◀ James Garfield was born in this log cabin in Ohio.

and Eliza Ballou Garfield—had moved their growing family to Orange Township from Newburgh, a town near Cleveland. Abram was a farmer and canal builder.

The little family was doing well until 1833, when Abram suddenly fell ill and died. Eliza was left with four young children to care for and no money. James, the youngest, was just eighteen months old.

Eliza Ballou Garfield raised four children on her own.

During the next few years, Eliza and her children worked hard to survive. James, his brother, and two sisters helped out on the 30-acre (12-hectare) farm. In his early teens, James began doing odd jobs at other farms to help earn money for the family.

Although the Garfields were always short of money, Eliza made sure that her children valued learning and education. When James was just three years old—too

◄ Young James
attended a nearby
school and loved
to read.

young to work—his sister carried him to a nearby
school. As he grew, James developed a love of reading.
He read anything and everything he could get his hands
on. James liked books about U.S. history. He also liked
adventure stories. He loved to read tales of sailors and
the sea.

When James was sixteen, he left home to become a sailor on Lake Erie. Instead, James got a job on the *Evening Star,* a barge that traveled the Ohio Canal. At first, he worked onshore, driving the mules that pulled the barge up and down the canal. Later he worked on the barge itself.

Sixteen-year-old James hoped to become a sailor once he reached Cleveland, Ohio.

Garfield driving mules that pulled the Evening Star *on the Ohio Canal*

James was a strong young man. He quickly proved his worth onboard the *Evening Star.* Before long, he was earning $14 a month. The work was hard and sometimes dangerous. James found himself floating in the canal a few times. He recalled that he nearly drowned about fourteen times!

James's career as a bargeman ended after just six weeks when he suddenly became very ill with **malaria.** People get malaria when they are bitten by a mosquito that carries the disease. James had to return home. He spent months recovering from his illness. While he lay in bed, James decided that the laborer's life was not for him.

In spring 1849, Eliza gave James $17—the family's entire savings—and sent him off to nearby Geauga Seminary. The high school run by Free Will Baptists was in Chester, just 10 miles (16 kilometers) from home. The seminary would satisfy James's thirst for knowledge. Over the next ten years, he devoted himself to a life of learning.

That $17 didn't last long, but James was determined to stay in school. He was willing to do any work that would earn the money to pay for his classes. And that he did! By working as a carpenter, a woodcutter, a farmer, and a teacher, James was able to pay for his own schooling.

Garfield worked ▶ hard to receive an education from Western Reserve Eclectic Institute, later called Hiram College.

In August 1851, James was admitted to the Western Reserve Eclectic Institute (later called Hiram College). The school was run by the Disciples of Christ, the religion that James belonged to. At the institute, James did well in **debating** and public speaking. Again, he decided to do whatever it took to get an education. James earned money to pay for his schooling in a variety of ways. Among other things, he taught English, Latin, Greek, drawing, penmanship, and worked as a carpenter.

In 1854, James attended Williams College, a well-known school in Massachusetts. Two years later, he graduated with high honors. He then returned to the Western

Reserve Eclectic Institute to teach Greek, Latin, and literature. James was a good teacher, and his students loved him. The college staff respected him as well, and in 1857, James was made the school's president. He was just twenty-six years old. At the Western Reserve Eclectic Institute, James also began to study law. In 1861, he became a lawyer.

In November 1858, James had married Lucretia "Crete" Rudolph. He met that intelligent young lady when they were both students at Geauga Seminary. Over the years, James came to rely on his wife as a friend and

companion. As a result, the pair became nearly inseparable.
They had seven children together, five of whom grew
to adulthood.

During the 1850s, James used his outstanding speaking skills to preach for the Disciples of Christ. He also
made public speeches attacking slavery. James was very
much against slavery. He called it "this giant evil."

At that time, slavery was part of life in the Southern
states, but it was against the law in the Northern states.
By the early 1860s, the conflict between the North and
the South over slavery was ready to explode into violence.

War Hero and Politician

★ ★ ★

At the time of the Civil War (1861–1865), two political parties dominated U.S. politics. The first was the Democratic Party. Most Democrats at that time thought states should be able to decide for themselves whether to allow slavery. The second important political party was the Republican Party. It had been founded in 1854. Republicans did not want to allow slavery in the new states and territories being established in the West.

After Garfield graduated from Williams College, he became a Republican. He quickly jumped into the world of politics. During the 1856 presidential election, Garfield campaigned for John C. Frémont, the Republican **candidate** from

▼ *John C. Frémont was a presidential candidate in the 1856 election.*

California. Like Garfield, Frémont was strongly against allowing slavery in the West. On Election Day, however, Frémont was defeated by Democrat James Buchanan.

Three years later, Garfield's name was put in nomination for a seat in the Ohio Senate. During the campaign, he spoke often about the evils of slavery. In a letter he wrote around that time, Garfield remarked that the sin of slavery would never be forgiven without the shedding of blood. Garfield easily won the election. He moved to Columbus, the capital of Ohio, to begin his new duties.

In 1860, Garfield campaigned for Republican presidential candidate Abraham Lincoln. Although he supported Lincoln in his run for president, Garfield did not always agree with Lincoln's policies.

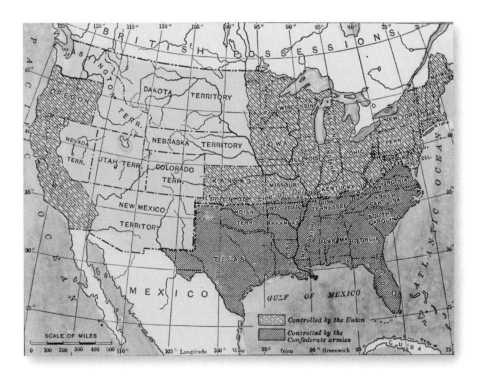

The Confederate states at the end of 1861

Lincoln won the election. Many Southerners were convinced that he would take steps to end slavery. As a result, Southern states began to leave the Union. South Carolina was the first to **secede,** in December 1860. Mississippi, Florida, Alabama, Georgia, Louisiana, and Texas followed. In February, these states joined together to form their own country called the Confederate States of America. By May, eleven states had joined the Confederacy.

Garfield was strongly against breaking up the Union. He believed that the U.S. government must use military force to stop the Southern states from leaving. Garfield began studying books to learn about great generals, battles, and military planning.

The American Civil War between the Northern states and the Southern states began in April 1861.

Garfield joined the Union, or Northern, army, eager to do his part. He convinced a number of his former students to join the army with him. Before long, Colonel Garfield and his men were ready for action.

Garfield's first taste of battle came in January 1862. At the Battle of

Garfield was eager to fight with the Union army.

Garfield's troops ▶ defeated the Confederates and maintained control of Kentucky.

Middle Creek in Kentucky, Garfield and his troops faced a Confederate force. Thanks to Garfield's brilliant planning, his forces were able to beat the Confederates and keep Kentucky under Union control. Because of that battle, President Lincoln promoted Garfield to brigadier general. At thirty years old, Garfield was now the youngest brigadier general in the army.

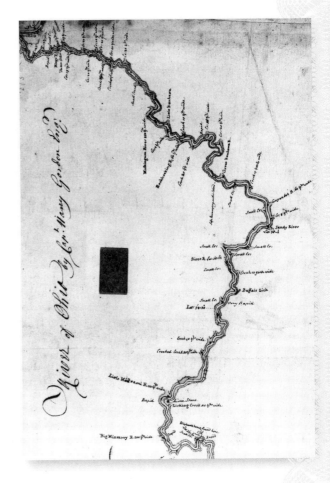

▲ *Garfield navigated the Ohio River to bring his men food and supplies.*

Over the next few months, Garfield's goal was to drive any Confederate troops out of eastern Kentucky and into Virginia. The days and weeks wore on. Garfield's troops began to run out of food and other supplies. Garfield headed to the Ohio River and took control of a steamship loaded with food and other **cargo.** He then steered the boat on a dangerous forty-eight-hour trip back to his men.

General Grant led the charge at Shiloh before Garfield and his troops joined him in that bloody battle.

In the spring of 1862, Garfield and his men marched from Kentucky into Tennessee to join General Ulysses S. Grant's men. They arrived just as the Battle of Shiloh was ending. That battle was one of the bloodiest of the Civil War. More than 10,000 soldiers on each side died during the two-day conflict. Garfield was horrified by the violence and the bloodshed.

Back home in Ohio, people heard of Garfield's bravery and daring wartime actions. Stories about his activities were printed in local and national newspapers. In October 1862, the people of Ohio elected Garfield to the U.S. House of Representatives. Garfield was flattered, but he didn't want to leave the army—yet.

Garfield's last Civil War battle was
the Battle of Chickamauga in September
1863. The Union army was beaten badly at this battle in
northeastern Georgia. Garfield sealed his reputation as a
war hero during this battle, however. He rode on horseback
along the front lines. There, in the face of heavy enemy fire,
he told General George Thomas what was happening to the
troops. His action saved the army from being destroyed.

▲ *Garfield was first a war hero at Chickamauga (left) and then became a congressman in Washington, D.C.*

After Chickamauga, Garfield was promoted to the rank
of major general. President Lincoln, however, believed that
Garfield would be most useful in Washington, D.C. He
convinced Garfield to leave the U.S. Army and take his seat
in Congress. Thus, in December 1863, more than a year
after his election, Garfield arrived in Washington.

Rising to the Top

★   ★   ★

Garfield was thirty-two years old when he entered the U.S. House of Representatives. Over the next seventeen years, he earned a reputation as an outstanding congressman. He was hardworking and intelligent. Garfield was reelected to the House eight times!

Republicans thought Garfield was one of their best and brightest. He was skilled at finding ways to help different groups within the Republican Party get along. One politician called Garfield "one of the most useful men ever in the . . . House."

Garfield's first year in Congress was a lonely one for him. Lucretia and the children had stayed behind in Ohio. In 1864, however, Garfield's family joined him in Washington, D.C. At first, the family lived in rented rooms. Then, in 1869, Garfield built a house for them in the capital. Garfield's mother also came along. She

spent winters in Washington with her son and his family.

In Congress, Garfield was one of a group of politicians known as Radical Republicans. They favored harsh treatment of the South after the Civil War. They thought the United States should seize the property of anyone who had helped the Confederacy. Like other Radical Republicans, Garfield thought that Confederate leaders should be killed or sent out of the country. He also favored

▲ *Garfield lived with his wife, children, and mother in this house in Washington, D.C.*

The House of ◄
Representatives
found President
Johnson guilty
on this bill of
impeachment.

allowing blacks to vote. In 1868, members of Congress voted to **impeach** President Andrew Johnson because they thought he was being too soft on the South. Johnson was the first U.S. president to be impeached, or charged with wrongdoing.

Garfield was very interested in the economic health of the nation. He wanted government loans to be paid back with gold, rather than silver or paper money. Garfield also worked to cut government spending.

Garfield favored ►
paying back gov-
ernment loans in
gold, as opposed
to using silver or
paper money, such
as this $10 bill
printed in 1869.

Over the years, Garfield became one of the most powerful men in the Republican Party. In 1876, his fellow Republicans chose him to be the Republican leader in the House of Representatives. This gave Garfield the chance to show off his superb writing and speaking skills.

Garfield served as a member of the board of the Smithsonian Institution.

During his nine terms in office, Garfield accomplished many things. He helped set up the U.S. Department of Education. He also helped move a bill through Congress that created the U.S. Geological Survey. The Geological Survey studies and maps the nation's lands. Garfield also supported education for the deaf and sat on the board of the Smithsonian Institution. The Smithsonian collects and displays treasures from American history.

Three times during his career in Congress, Garfield was touched by scandal. Each time, he was accused of taking bribes. Garfield fiercely denied any wrongdoing, and the charges against him were never proved. More importantly, the charges did not stop voters in Ohio from reelecting Garfield. In 1880, Ohio legislators elected Garfield to represent Ohio in the U.S. Senate. Before he could take his seat, however, something even more important happened in his career: the Republican Party chose Garfield to run for president. His **nomination** was a surprise to many people, including Garfield himself!

Three Republicans had wanted to be the Republican candidate for president. One was war hero and former president Ulysses S. Grant. The second was Senator James G. Blaine of Maine. The third was Secretary of the Treasury John Sherman of Ohio.

Garfield supported Sherman. He agreed to head Sherman's campaign

and to speak for him at the Republican **convention** in
Chicago. Some Republicans at the convention began to
think that Garfield himself wanted to be president. When
he gave a speech supporting Sherman, it took fifteen
minutes before he even mentioned Sherman's name!

As it happened, none of the three candidates had
enough support to win the nomination. The convention
dragged on and on. After six days and thirty-three **ballots,**
no candidate was the clear favorite.

Finally, on the thirty-fourth ballot, sixteen Republicans
cast their votes for Garfield. A ripple of shock ran through

◄ *The 1880
Republican
Convention in
Chicago*

the crowd. Support for Garfield grew rapidly. On the thirty-sixth ballot, he was declared the Republican candidate for president. Chester A. Arthur of New York was chosen to run for vice president.

The Democratic candidate for president was Winfield S. Hancock of Pennsylvania. Hancock was a war hero who had fought for the Union during the Civil War. After the war, he had served as the military governor of Louisiana and Texas. Unlike Garfield, though, Hancock had never worked in politics. During the election, the Republicans made much of Hancock's lack of political experience.

A campaign poster ▶ for Democrat Winfield S. Hancock and running mate William Hayden English

The campaign became nasty. Democrats brought up the old charges about Garfield taking bribes. Yet the Republicans were willing to play dirty, too. They charged that Hancock had planned to march to Washington during the war and throw President Lincoln out of office.

At the same time, Republicans talked about Garfield's humble childhood in a log cabin. They praised his bravery on the battlefield and his brilliant career in Congress. They wrote campaign biographies. Garfield was the first presidential candidate to campaign in two languages. In Cleveland, Ohio, home of many German immigrants, Garfield gave speeches in German.

On Election Day, 80 percent of all U.S. voters went to the polls to select the next president. When the results were in, Garfield had defeated his opponent by fewer than 10,000 votes. It remains one

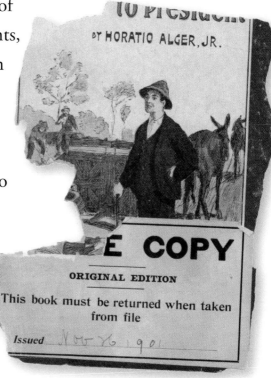

▼ *A tattered cover of the biography* From Canal Boy to President, *written shortly after Garfield's death*

A Republican banner in support of James Garfield and Chester A. Arthur

A political cartoon of a triumphant Garfield riding an American eagle

of the closest presidential elections in U.S. history. Garfield did better in the electoral college, where he defeated Hancock 214 to 155. The electoral college is the group of people in each state chosen to elect the president and vice president.

After winning the election, Garfield left Congress. He seemed almost sad to be taking the nation's top job. He knew that being president would set him apart from many of his friends and coworkers. Garfield imagined the presidency as a "bleak mountain." He had reached the top, but he would stand there alone.

Short Stay in the White House

★   ★   ★

After the election, Garfield stayed on his farm in Mentor, Ohio. He began preparing for his family's move to the White House. Even before he took office, however, he learned that the president's job was not easy. Hundreds of people visited Garfield. Each visitor hoped to get a job in Garfield's new administration.

Garfield's **inauguration** was held on March 4, 1881. In the speech he gave that day, he talked about the rights of black citizens. He called their release from slavery "the most important political change . . . since the adoption of the **Constitution.**"

▼ Garfield was sworn in as president in 1881.

Garfield's family, including his eighty-year-old mother, Eliza, attended his inauguration. Eliza Garfield was the first mother to watch her son be sworn in as president. She moved into the White House with Garfield, Lucretia, and

Like his wife and mother, Garfield's children also attended his inauguration.

◄ *The White House around the time Garfield and his family lived there*

their five children. Eliza, who always dressed in black, spent most of her time in her bedroom. At dinnertime, her son walked downstairs to the dining room with her.

Lucretia had big plans for the White House. She wanted to restore the White House furniture. Just two months after moving in, however, Lucretia became ill with malaria. She was sent to the New Jersey seashore to recover.

As president, Garfield quickly settled into a daily routine. He arose each day at 7 A.M. While eating breakfast, he read the morning newspapers. By 10 A.M., the president began meeting with the public. Garfield dreaded the afternoons, however. He thought they were a waste of time because each day he had to deal with the hundreds of people who crowded the White House halls, hoping for a government job.

Garfield was frustrated by this process of the president handing out government jobs. "My day is frittered away by the personal seeking of people," he said, "when it ought to be given to the great problem[s] which concern the whole country." Later, Garfield complained even more bitterly about the president's job, "My God! What is there in this place that a man should ever want to get into it?"

Senator Roscoe ▼ Conkling

Garfield was also hounded by various groups within his own Republican Party. One group, the Stalwarts, was led by Senator Roscoe Conkling of New York. Vice President Chester Arthur was also a Stalwart. Conkling and his group were used to holding a lot of power within the party. Soon, Conkling began to put pressure on Garfield to place Stalwarts in important jobs.

VOL. VIII.–No. 208.   MARCH 2, 1881.   Price, 10 Cents.

"What fools these Mortals be!"
MIDSUMMER-NIGHTS DREAM

Puck

PUBLISHED BY
KEPPLER & SCHWARZMANN.   NEW YORK   OFFICE No. 21 – 23 WARREN ST
TRADE MARK REGISTERED 1878.
"ENTERED AT THE POST OFFICE AT NEW YORK, AND ADMITTED FOR TRANSMISSION THROUGH THE MAILS AT SECOND CLASS RATES."

◀ *A political cartoon pokes fun at rival senators Blaine and Conkling, with Garfield binding them together.*

Garfield refused to be swayed by Conkling, however. Although he did give some jobs to the Stalwarts, he chose the men he wanted. One of his appointments was Senator James G. Blaine from Maine. Garfield chose Blaine, an

The honesty of U.S. mail carriers was called into question in the Star Route Affair.

enemy of Conkling's, to be secretary of state. He also appointed enemies of Conkling to other important jobs. Conkling quit the Senate in disgust.

In March, Garfield had Thomas James, his postmaster general, begin investigating a scandal in the Post Office. Called the Star Route Affair, the scandal involved mail routes in remote areas of the West and Southwest. These routes, traveled by mail carriers on horseback or in wagons, were called star routes. The mail carriers often over-charged the government for their services. By 1880, more than $6 million was being paid each year to people working the star routes.

As president, Garfield showed that he was carefully watching the nation's financial health. One of his major accomplishments was to lower the interest rate the U.S. government paid on some savings bonds. By doing this, Garfield saved the United States about $10 million a year.

▲ Secretary of the Treasury William Windom of Minnesota worked with the president to improve the nation's financial situation.

No one knows what else Garfield might have done as president. In July, Garfield began to prepare for a family trip to Massachusetts. Little did he know that his time in office was coming to an end.

A Violent End to a Brilliant Career

★ ★ ★

On the morning of July 2, 1881, President James A. Garfield entered a Washington railroad station. Garfield and his two oldest sons, Harry and Jim, were planning to visit Williams College. The two boys were outside the station when they heard shots ring out.

The gun used ▶
to kill Garfield

Inside the station, Garfield cried, "My God! What is that?" and fell to the floor. He had been shot twice from behind. The first bullet grazed his arm. The second bullet entered his back and lodged itself about 3.5 inches (9 centimeters) from his spine.

The shooter was Charles J. Guiteau, a mentally disturbed man who had a history of violence. Guiteau had wanted Garfield to give him a government job in France, but he was turned away. For days before the shooting, Guiteau had stalked the president. He had originally planned to kill Garfield on June 18, but he put off the killing when he saw that the president's wife was with him.

Guiteau didn't try to escape after shooting the president. Police officers who searched his pockets found a letter addressed to the White House. In the letter,

▲ *President Garfield's assassin, Charles Guiteau*

Guiteau wrote that he had shot Garfield to "unite the Republican Party and save the Republic."

Garfield was taken back to the White House. When Lucretia, in New Jersey, learned of the shooting, she quickly returned to Washington.

Over the next few weeks, the world waited for news of Garfield's condition. One doctor after another was brought in to examine the president.

Some of Garfield's doctors accidentally made his wound worse.

Most of the doctors, however, only made matters worse. The first doctor to examine the president stuck his finger—and instruments that were not perfectly clean— into the wound. The doctor was trying to find the bullet. He only managed to make the wound bigger.

Other doctors performed similar "exams," and Garfield's wound became infected. The president suffered greatly. He was in constant pain. Historians today believe that if Garfield had received better treatment—or had been left alone—he probably would have recovered.

In a desperate effort to find the bullet in Garfield's body, doctors brought in Alexander Graham Bell, the

◄ Garfield's family tried to comfort him during his final days.

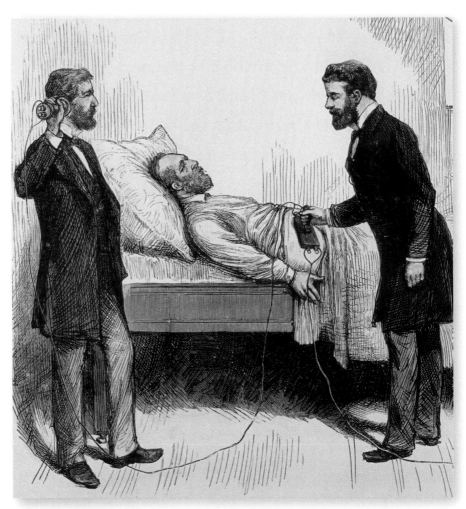

Alexander Graham ▶
Bell (right) used his
metal detector
to search for the
bullet inside
Garfield's body.

inventor of the telephone. Bell had recently created a
metal detector. The machine, however, was of no help in
finding the bullet. The alarm went off no matter what
part of Garfield's body it was near. Later, people realized
that the metal springs in the president's mattress had set
off the alarm.

On September 6, Garfield was taken by train to Francklyn Cottage near the seashore in Elberon, New Jersey. Doctors wanted to get him out of the brutal heat of Washington, D.C., and into the healing ocean breezes. A special set of railroad tracks had been laid down to carry

◄ *Special track was laid so that Garfield could be safely transported from the capital to the seaside house in New Jersey.*

the president to the door of the seaside house. In New Jersey, the president seemed to be recovering. Suddenly, however, he became much worse. As he lay in bed, Garfield spoke of his assassin. "He must have been crazy," the president said. "None but an insane person could have done such a thing. What could he have wanted to shoot me for?"

On September 19, 1881, nearly eleven weeks after he had been shot, President James A. Garfield died. Garfield,

Garfield died on September 19, 1881.

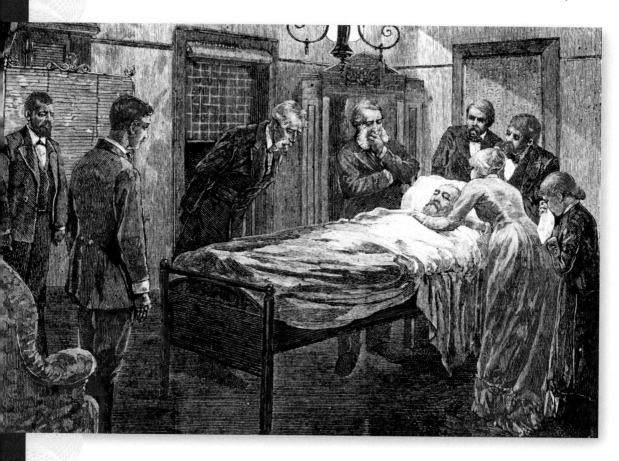

just forty-nine years old, had spent just fewer than two hundred days in office, eighty of them in his sickbed.

For two days, Garfield's body lay in the Capitol, where he had served so long and so faithfully. Thousands of citizens passed through the building to pay their last respects to the slain president. Then Garfield's coffin was taken by train to Ohio, his home state.

◄ *Americans paid their final respects to President James Garfield in the Capitol.*

Charles J. Guiteau was later tried for killing Garfield. Throughout his trial, he claimed that it was Garfield's doctors who had really killed the president.

The trial of Charles ▼
Guiteau (standing)

The jury did not agree. They found Guiteau guilty. He was executed by hanging in June 1882.

Garfield had little time to make a difference as president. Historians are unsure of how successful he might have been had he finished his term. Garfield's death brought one very important change, though. In 1883, President Chester Arthur signed a bill that helped change the way people are chosen for government jobs.

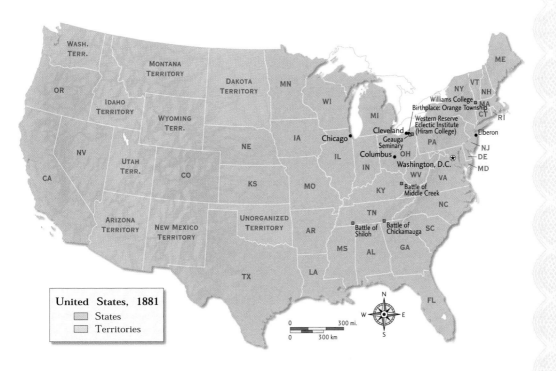

United States, 1881
- States
- Territories

Although Garfield's presidency was cut short, his life still serves as an example of how far a person can go when he is determined to succeed.

On the day of ▶ Garfield's funeral, railroad workers held a memorial service by the Toltec Tunnel near the border of New Mexico and Colorado. They later had this granite monument built to honor the slain president.

GLOSSARY

★ ★ ★

assassin—someone who murders an important politician

ballots—votes

candidate—someone running for office in an election

cargo—products carried by ship

Constitution—the document stating the basic laws of the United States

convention—a large meeting during which a political party chooses its candidates

debating—formal discussions

impeach—to charge a public official with a serious crime

inauguration—a president's swearing-in ceremony

malaria—a disease that causes fever and chills; it is spread by the bite of mosquitoes that carry the disease

nomination—chosen as a candidate for office

secede—withdraw from

JAMES ABRAM GARFIELD'S LIFE AT A GLANCE

★ ★ ★

PERSONAL

Born:	November 19, 1831
Father's name:	Abram Garfield
Mother's name:	Eliza Ballou Garfield
Education:	Graduated from Williams College in 1856
Wife's name:	Lucretia Rudolph Garfield (1832–1918)
Married:	November 11, 1858
Children:	Eliza A. Garfield (1860–1863); Harry A. Garfield (1863–1942); James R. Garfield (1865–1950); Mary Garfield (1867–1947); Irvin M. Garfield (1870–1951); Abram Garfield (1872–1958); Edward Garfield (1874–1876)
Died:	September 19, 1881, in Elberon, New Jersey
Buried:	Cleveland, Ohio

PUBLIC

Occupation before presidency:	Teacher, preacher, college president, politician, lawyer
Occupation after presidency:	None
Military service:	Major general during the Civil War
Other government positions:	Member of the Ohio state senate; representative from Ohio in the U.S. House of Representatives
Political party:	Republican
Vice president:	Chester A. Arthur
Dates in office:	March 4, 1881– September 19, 1881
Presidential opponent:	Winfield Scott Hancock (Democrat)
Number of votes (Electoral College):	4,453,295 of 8,867,377 (214 of 369)
Writings:	None

James A. Garfield's Cabinet

Secretary of state:
James G. Blaine (1881)

Secretary of the treasury:
William Windom (1881)

Secretary of war:
Robert Todd Lincoln (1881)

Attorney general:
I. Wayne McVeagh (1881)

Postmaster general:
Thomas L. James (1881)

Secretary of the navy:
William H. Hunt (1881)

Secretary of the interior:
Samuel J. Kirkwood (1881)

JAMES ABRAM GARFIELD'S LIFE AND TIMES

★ ★ ★

GARFIELD'S LIFE

November 19, Garfield is born in a log cabin near Cleveland, Ohio — 1831

Eliza Garfield (above) gives her son the family's savings and sends him off to attend Geauga Academy — 1849

WORLD EVENTS

1833 — Great Britain abolishes slavery

1836 — Texans defeat Mexican troops at San Jacinto after a deadly battle at the Alamo (below)

1840

1840 — Auguste Rodin, famous sculptor of *The Thinker* (below), is born

GARFIELD'S LIFE

Studies and teaches at 1851–
Western Reserve Eclectic 1854
Institute (now Hiram
College) (below)

Graduates with honors 1856
from Williams College
(above)

1850

WORLD EVENTS

1852   American Harriet
Beecher Stowe (below)
publishes *Uncle
Tom's Cabin*

1856   Electrical scientist and
inventor Nikola Tesla is
born

Gregor Mendel starts his
research on genetics

GARFIELD'S LIFE

WORLD EVENTS

Becomes president of   1857
Western Reserve
Eclectic Institute

Marries Lucretia   1858
Rudolph (below)

1858   English scientist
Charles Darwin
(above) presents his
theory of evolution

India comes under
the direct rule of
Great Britain

Famous opera
composer Giacomo
Buccini is born in
Lucca, Italy

GARFIELD'S LIFE

WORLD EVENTS

Elected to Ohio
State Senate 1859

1860 1860 Austrian composer
Gustav Mahler
(above) is born
in Kalischt (now in
Austria)

Joins Union army to 1861
fight in the Civil War
(below)

1861 Jefferson Davis is
named president
of the Confederate
States of America

Kansas becomes
the thirty-fourth
U.S. state as others
are leaving to join
the Confederacy

GARFIELD'S LIFE

Resigns from Union 1863
army to enter the U.S.
House of Represen-
tatives (below)

Becomes Republican 1876
leader in the House of
Representatives

WORLD EVENTS

1865   *Tristan and Isolde,* by
German composer
Richard Wagner,
opens in Munich

Lewis Carroll writes *Alice's
Adventures in Wonderland*

1868   Louisa May Alcott
publishes *Little Women*

1869   The periodic table of
elements is invented

The transcontinental
railroad across the United
States is completed (below)

1870

1870   John D. Rockefeller
founds the Standard
Oil Company

1876   The Battle of the Little
Bighorn is a victory
for Native Americans
defending their homes
in the West against
General George Custer

Alexander Graham Bell
uses the first telephone
to speak to his assistant,
Thomas Watson

GARFIELD'S LIFE

WORLD EVENTS

1877   German inventor Nikolaus A. Otto works on what will become the internal combustion engine for automobiles

1879   Electric lights are invented

Elected to the U.S. Senate; later that year becomes the Republican candidate for president   1880

July 2, shot by Charles J. Guiteau in a Washington, D.C., railroad station   1881

September 19, dies of an infection in his wound; Chester Arthur becomes president

1881   Former slave Booker T. Washington opens Tuskegee Institute, a college for African-Americans

1882   Thomas Edison opens the first electric power station in New York City

UNDERSTANDING JAMES ABRAM GARFIELD AND HIS PRESIDENCY

★ ★ ★

IN THE LIBRARY

Brunelli, Carol. *James A. Garfield, Our Twentieth President.*
Chanhassen, Minn.: The Child's World, 2001.

Joseph, Paul. *James A. Garfield.*
Minneapolis: Abdo Publishers, 2000.

ON THE WEB

For more information on this topic, use FactHound.

1. Go to *www.facthound.com*
2. Type in this book ID: 0756502675
3. Click on the *Fetch It* button.

FactHound will find the best Web sites for you.

GARFIELD HISTORIC SITES
ACROSS THE COUNTRY

James A. Garfield Birthplace
Route 91
Moreland Hills, OH 44022
440/247-7282
To see a replica log cabin and the spot
where Garfield's original cabin stood

James A. Garfield Monument
Lake View Cemetery
12316 Euclid Avenue
Cleveland, OH 44106
216/421-2665
To visit Garfield's grave and receive
a tour of the grounds

James A. Garfield National Historic Site
8095 Mentor Avenue
Mentor, OH 44060
440/255-8722
To see the home where Garfield and his family
lived before he became president

THE U.S. PRESIDENTS
(Years in Office)

★ ★ ★

1. **George Washington**
   (March 4, 1789-March 3, 1797)
2. **John Adams**
   (March 4, 1797-March 3, 1801)
3. **Thomas Jefferson**
   (March 4, 1801-March 3, 1809)
4. **James Madison**
   (March 4, 1809-March 3, 1817)
5. **James Monroe**
   (March 4, 1817-March 3, 1825)
6. **John Quincy Adams**
   (March 4, 1825-March 3, 1829)
7. **Andrew Jackson**
   (March 4, 1829-March 3, 1837)
8. **Martin Van Buren**
   (March 4, 1837-March 3, 1841)
9. **William Henry Harrison**
   (March 6, 1841-April 4, 1841)
10. **John Tyler**
    (April 6, 1841-March 3, 1845)
11. **James K. Polk**
    (March 4, 1845-March 3, 1849)
12. **Zachary Taylor**
    (March 5, 1849-July 9, 1850)
13. **Millard Fillmore**
    (July 10, 1850-March 3, 1853)
14. **Franklin Pierce**
    (March 4, 1853-March 3, 1857)
15. **James Buchanan**
    (March 4, 1857-March 3, 1861)
16. **Abraham Lincoln**
    (March 4, 1861-April 15, 1865)
17. **Andrew Johnson**
    (April 15, 1865-March 3, 1869)

18. **Ulysses S. Grant**
    (March 4, 1869-March 3, 1877)
19. **Rutherford B. Hayes**
    (March 4, 1877-March 3, 1881)
20. **James Garfield**
    (March 4, 1881-Sept 19, 1881)
21. **Chester Arthur**
    (Sept 20, 1881-March 3, 1885)
22. **Grover Cleveland**
    (March 4, 1885-March 3, 1889)
23. **Benjamin Harrison**
    (March 4, 1889-March 3, 1893)
24. **Grover Cleveland**
    (March 4, 1893-March 3, 1897)
25. **William McKinley**
    (March 4, 1897-
    September 14, 1901)
26. **Theodore Roosevelt**
    (September 14, 1901-
    March 3, 1909)
27. **William Howard Taft**
    (March 4, 1909-March 3, 1913)
28. **Woodrow Wilson**
    (March 4, 1913-March 3, 1921)
29. **Warren G. Harding**
    (March 4, 1921-August 2, 1923)
30. **Calvin Coolidge**
    (August 3, 1923-March 3, 1929)
31. **Herbert Hoover**
    (March 4, 1929-March 3, 1933)
32. **Franklin D. Roosevelt**
    (March 4, 1933-April 12, 1945)

33. **Harry S. Truman**
    (April 12, 1945-
    January 20, 1953)
34. **Dwight D. Eisenhower**
    (January 20, 1953-
    January 20, 1961)
35. **John F. Kennedy**
    (January 20, 1961-
    November 22, 1963)
36. **Lyndon B. Johnson**
    (November 22, 1963-
    January 20, 1969)
37. **Richard M. Nixon**
    (January 20, 1969-
    August 9, 1974)
38. **Gerald R. Ford**
    (August 9, 1974-
    January 20, 1977)
39. **James Earl Carter**
    (January 20, 1977-
    January 20, 1981)
40. **Ronald Reagan**
    (January 20, 1981-
    January 20, 1989)
41. **George H. W. Bush**
    (January 20, 1989-
    January 20, 1993)
42. **William Jefferson Clinton**
    (January 20, 1993-
    January 20, 2001)
43. **George W. Bush**
    (January 20, 2001-)

INDEX

★   ★   ★

Index

ABOUT THE AUTHOR

Robin S. Doak has been writing for children for more than fourteen years. A former editor of *Weekly Reader* and *U*S*Kids* magazine, Ms. Doak has authored fun and educational materials for kids of all ages. Some of her work includes biographies of explorers such as Henry Hudson and John Smith, as well as other titles in this series. Ms. Doak is a past winner of an Educational Press Association of America Distinguished Achievement Award. She lives with her husband and three children in central Connecticut.